The Language of Crows

Lorrie Wolfe

The Language of Crows
©Lorrie Wolfe, 2024

Books may be purchased in quantity and/or special sales by contacting the publisher. All inquiries related to such matters should be addressed to:

Middle Creek Publishing & Audio
9161 Pueblo Mountain Park Road
Beulah, CO 81023
editor@middlecreekpublishing.com
(719) 369-9050

First Paperback Edition, 2024
ISBN: 978-1-957483-22-1
Cover Art: selection from an AI Generated image, edited and altered.
Cover Design: David Anthony Martin, Middle Creek Publishing & Audio
Author Image: Aron Wolfe

The Language of Crows

Lorrie Wolfe

Middle Creek Publishing & Audio
Beulah, CO   USA

For Steve ~
Thank you for giving me wings

Table of Contents

Creation

> *In the beginning, the earth*
> *was unformed and void...*
> —Genesis

On the first day, I was a child
playing alone in the sandbox.

On the second day, I met you, and the world
shifted   just a little.

On the third, we conceived sons who were born
in great waves of wonder.

On the fourth, they grew tall and waved goodbye
as they left for college and the world.

And on the fifth, we held grandchildren
high in the air

and measured their progress in pencil
on the closet doorframe.

On the sixth day, we grew gray, wrote poems,
and went for walks that took forty years.

On the seventh day, we rested
on memories and laurels and riverbanks.

      And whatever shall we do
      next week, my dear?

Hummingbird *pas de deux*

Oh, Muse—
listen,
you forgot the hummingbird
when you handed out songs.

Instead, you bestowed
wings
thrumming
three thousand times a minute,

whirring tailfeathers in showy dive,
careening
a desperate downthrust
of iridescence

risking the splash of bright death
on a highway below,
wheeling up just in time
to hover before the desired mate.

I wanted to love you like that.

September Morning

Unexpected first frost,
the lightest glaze
across the field,

a fine line drawn down the ruckled trunk
of the old cottonwood,
a beard that was not there yesterday.

Amid bursts of fire and fuchsia,
summer's last revel splayed
in final fevered abandon,

sumac, like the reddened lips
of a teenage girl,
quivers with anticipation.

I see an icy arc, fragile and quick,
in a color not used
these five months.

It drifts like Egyptian gauze
across the pale gold grasses
along the ditches.

Tender cosmos bend their heads
and poplars drop golden tributes
one by one by one.

Autumn Serenade for Lorca

In summer, even the wind is green.
Heat-drenched August
stretches out its green arms,
but September knows what storms
sear them and snap them.

Oh! glorious fall, this final flare,
as aspens, ablaze, spill golden coins
in a treasure of leaving.
One last flame
before the inevitable ashes.

This bright interlude
ends its seductive tango,
the passionate flicks of
trumpet vine's fervid tangle
give way to the
heaving relief of fruit trees
releasing ripened burdens.

Green, how I want you green.
But, where has my green summer fled?
Green has become yesterday's fleeting fancy,
a passion longed for, like an exaltation of larks
now locked away.

Tomorrow, rain songs begin their soft refrain.
Residue of green's bright dreams
will be reduced to dun, ochre,
umber, and gray.

Lean closer, listen for just one note,
a final crack and crunch as dry leaves
sound autumn's brief serenade.

Fall envies summer.
Verde que te quiero verde
Green, how I wanted you green.

October First

October and the light is fading,
the day's last feeble glow blazed and spent.
Dusk comes too soon. Memory of summer abides
and cool autumn is a disappointment.

Still I search each afternoon for one more
fiery fling, a last crimson page not yet turned to dry rot,
hoping for a passionate red or sprightly yellow
where so much green leafage used to riot.

Snow has not yet arrived to soften the blow.
White veils flung from dun clouds would be a relief
after struggling to find color and delight,
where summer's star has met sunshine's thief.

How vain—this attempt to hang on to a season
past its prime—is beyond all reason.

Not Writing at the Lake in October

Along the live green edge of the lake
translucent tufts of white foam
gather and ruffle.
Beside me, my husband,
in tee shirt and jaunty red cap

perches in his lawn chair,
oblivious to high-altitude wind,
absorbed in watching
for the tiniest movement of pole-tip,
ready to spring, tug, and scroll.

I am not a fisherman.
I sit layered in sweatshirt,
winter jacket and heavy socks,
muffler doubled and tucked,
an old wool hat pulled over my ears.

With fingers almost too numb
to grasp a pen,
distracted by motion of mosses
and dreams of hot cocoa,
my eyes drift from paper to stratused sky.

This rare mid-week respite is an escape
from our workaday drone,
a last thin huzzah of sun
before fall turns
relentlessly toward winter.

I endure this wind for the chilly pleasures
of hearing water sip
into slips of shore-grasses,
a snap of pine
whipping bright mountain air,

and for a possible glimpse
of a liquid rainbow trout
as it arcs in terrified, breathless leaps
to unhook—
        a lake-sacrifice for our supper.

I persevere despite my desire for solitude
and a thermostat I can adjust
for the sake of this quiet man
whose gentle ministrations
 to worm, hook, tackle,

whose concentration on such details
and kindness to the blessed fish,
confirm what I already know—
he will be equally patient, and warm,
when he returns his attention to me.

The Language of Crows

When you are far
I hear you in the language of crows
calling dawn into the lightening sky,
inky night distilled
into feathers, wings,
onyx eye.

In memory, I see you
clamber across branches
after chittering squirrels
and teasing crows.
Watch your feet, I say,
a talisman against broken bones.

That little boy has flown.
Now you can name every muscle
and bone that held you strong,
high enough to see the whole world
as you perched
in the maple's red canopy.

You are fully fledged.
Now the mountain holds you,
bestows its old knowledge
to your fingers, your sinews.
Listen, it says. *I will tell you
what you have always wanted to know*

*in the language of seasons,
of tea,
of silence.*
When words fail
I still hear you
in the language of crows.

A View from the Condo

I.

I sit on my small balcony
in the early shadows
shivering a little
from my night-time thoughts

or maybe just the cold.
Somewhere over a horizon
littered by buildings, the sun breaks,
pinking the sky for a glorious moment.

Thirty feet beyond the square patios,
the little scratches of gardens,
the ditch emerges like a secret jewel,
gray, then gold, then green,

a highway for birds and small-footed creatures,
sustenance for the cottonwood, deeply rooted.

II.

These banks have held for a hundred years.
This morning, water   glints   gurgles.
A red fox high-steps, silent
through the lightening grasses.

He's all black-tipped ears,
rotating, twitching,
narrow nose alert
to fenced dogs still asleep.

Depending on the wind,
he might catch the murmur
of a paddling mallard
or his duck-wife at rest among the reeds

unaware of the possibility
of becoming his foxy breakfast.

Sonnet for the Dead Days

—for the winter solstice

These are the dead days, so they say,
darkness early and sunrise late.
Don't stir, don't attract the gods' attention.
Hide your light under that bushel, don't mention

the name of your desire, lest it be taken
and your love be gone, your hope forsaken
or they take you for an enemy, on heresy bent,
and strike you dead for their own amusement.

These are the dead days, till the solstice sun climbs
its way through cloudbank. Only then, divine
to fathom the mind of the holy ones, their vision.
Atone for all past sins, of omission and commission.

On these gray days, when your lonely heart yearns,
plan your kindnesses for the day the light returns.

In January

Such audacity! This bone-cold month, redeemed
by birdsong when I least expect it,
improbable cantatas inspiring renewed resolutions.

I vow to lose weight, rise earlier,
give up chocolate and late-night television,
incorporate kale into every soup.

Oh brave unnamable bird, I thank you
even while we both know
your hopeful song cannot last.

The spattered roadside snow not melted,
the gutters are runneled with ice,
tomorrow's sky guaranteed gray again.

Spring is not yet the wisp of a dream,
but today a small brown bird
is singing Glorias! outside my window.

A Slight Warming Trend

Grief wraps my limbs in February chill
while its gray heft lies thick and still.
Fresh snow clinging to the sharpened pines
forms smatterings of green and white designs.

I wondered how long my grief would stay
when burdened by the dark of winter days.
Morning sun: the ice shattered. I stepped out
and let the bounty overcome my doubt.

Icy thoughts fade beneath this day's small sun
and slow release continues once begun.
Icicles cast reflections as they drip
and hope catches the light on every tip.

A prism's array brightens this small copse
while memory glows, and falls, with each drop.

How Women Go Mad

Wyoming has the nation's highest suicide rate:
mental health professionals blame it on the wind.

This banshee wind, will it never stop?
There's nothing out here to break it.
It blows away my every thought.
Just how long can a person take it?

Out here on the plains, nothing will break it.
With its endless whoosh and roar
it shakes me but I can't shake it.
It's uprooted a cottonwood, laid it across my door.

It blows away my every thought,
torn up and wrenched with whoosh and roar.
I am disjointed, though rest and sleep I've sought,
like the ruckled cottonwood, blocking my front door.

This wild wind brings terror and bluster.
I am disjointed from the peace I've sought.
My teeth taste of grit and dust, and what's more,
my hat's a wind-blown bag, and like it, I'm caught.

Branches and root-ball, exposed like dark petticoats,
wind bellows, every thought escaping,
and that eerie, sudden silence between gusts—
there is madness in that waiting.

Here it comes, that demonic whoosh and roar.
Then, suspense: is it over? The volume drops
to a whisper, then nothing, no slamming door.
IT'S BACK!
Oh this damned wind   will it never   stop?

In Unjust Spring

In Colorado the world is snow and un-snow.
April is filled with unpredictability,
enough to trick tender
apple blossoms to emerge too soon

and risk falling onto flakes,
piled deep and heavy
enough to break branches just
spiraling into green tender leaves.

Spring mornings are wet and chilly,
followed by hopeful afternoons.
Sun whispers zephyrs.
We will whether this weather.

Children shed their coats
into slushy-puddles, dancing
where just yesterday they tiptoed
gingerly onto crackling ice.

Colorado, yes unjust,
but by May or maybe June,
relentless Spring
always wins this battle with winter.

Wait for it!

Flowerbox

If she knew how to pray
she would do it now,
patting seeds into soil
between clods raked small and then sprinkled.
Each morning, she seeks a green sprout.
How long would it take?
At nine, she believed in nothing.
She had not yet seen shoots begin to flower
or found something to love
and had no understanding
of what either would demand from her.

The Seed's Prayer

I would be grateful
for even a small place
in the work of the world.

I would transform myself,
and become other
than what I am now.

I would shed the cotyledon shell
of my hardened heart,
and reach into its rooting darkness.

I know my plumate's leafy purpose
and will play my role in perfect faith
as I take one last green stretch.

I was once the heart of a flower.
Now I will serve below the earth's surface.
Before the flower freshly rises, I will be gone.

Come Rain or Come Shine

The lake sprouts goslings among the rushes.
Water, shriven of ice, cracks, realigns.
Gamboling children shed their Mackintoshes
as puddle-wonderful worlds fill their minds.

Snow forgiven, tulips stretch cups of red
warmed by the suddenly hopeful pale sunshine.
Each arcs to reach the sun-god overhead
while the piney beach is by spring's fine hand defined.

Reflecting a sky of cloudy piqué cotton,
water stipples, its azure caps aligned.
When winter's last bitter song's forgotten,
Colorado, I'm in your web entwined.

Though often fooled, lulled by false spring's design,
I'm still gonna' love you, like nobody's loved you,
                    come rain or come shine.*

Song by Johnny Mercer and Harold Arlen

They Are There Again

I.
as I drive into the dusk after your funeral rites,
the mated pair high on a single dead branch,
their great black bodies,
necks hulked into massive shoulders,

perfectly matching white heads,
raptor beaks yellow as yolk,
unforgiving round eyes that never
miss a movement below

catch the last golden rays
of western sun. They are so still
they might be carved into the tree
except for the silver trunk,

ruckled as only cottonwood can be,
its tangle of branches grim with winter.
This leafless bower is owned by two,
ceded by all smaller birds who know

this perfect perch is no longer
an open territory.
They turn their regal heads, each searching,
together yet independent.

II.
Slowly the male shuffles his bright talons
ruffles his black socks,
gripping, un-gripping, not quite resettling.
Suddenly he lurches more than leaps,

trusting his heavy body to wind and wings.
He powers into open air as they beat
once, twice, stroke by stroke, he circles
higher than I can see. Will he return?

I know that you will not, cannot.
On their branch, his mate
maintains her vigil, keeps the watch
as night hurtles in.

Great Blue Heron Rising

Dusky sun slants on slow, gray water.
A ruffling in the brush, a swoop of air,
a delft raincloud raises its fringed cape
and pulls forward as pewter wings arc and flare.

A form, ancient and wild, rises. Gangling legs
trail as leathered sinews stretch.
Prussian-hued feathers, fold, sweep, extend,
hunched shoulders reach, recoil into the ess-ed neck.

As the great blue bird bursts gravity's bounds
the golden beak arrows toward the low horizon,
one thin black streak streams back from the crest.
Narrow head tilts, a great lift has begun.

He makes for the cobalt clouds.
The wing does its work.

Snow Day with Diamonds

May 20, 2019

Frilly-edged tulips are in full bloom.
Lilacs sport their jeweled purple crowns.
Afternoon roils in, gray and gusty.
Streetlights come on early.
This is spring in Colorado.

Before dawn, I wake to a city gone silent.
Snow has begun, blanketing blossoms and rooftops.
Six inches of wet clumps and windblown drifts
fracture huge leafed-out branches
and snap young stems with impunity.

In May, hope is a dangerous act.

But hope rises anyway.
May flowers thrust their greening tips
up to the sun, relentless.
Such is the triumph of perennial youth
over long experience.

May plays the trickster.
But where is the joy in constancy?
Snow that sparkles with diamonds darkens.
Love changes.
Even if not as quickly as the weather

I will have to replant.

How Many Birds are Enough?

How many birds are too many to lose?
This is not a poem about birds.

Even when the world turns upside down
and we are alone nesting in our houses for too long,

turtle doves and partridges in pear trees,
where have they gone? Can we coax them back?

I cannot speak in their tongues. Let the birds pause
in their songs to hear my urgent silence.

In fifty years, we have lost three billion birds—
too many to count on a Christmas morning.

I cannot imagine even one billion no longer winging.
Is our human loss less imaginable?

My life-list will be forever incomplete.
How many ways have I been party to this disruption?

It seems impossible to atone for the passing
of even one robin or for the forgotten thrum

of hummingbirds in *pas de deux*,
dancing before the red feeder.

While God's eye is on the sparrow,
who looks after the passenger pigeon?

Who sees the tiny screech owl's flight,
so fleeting in its eastern woods?

There is a sanctity between plant, bird, and human,
a communion with leaves and feathers lifted aloft.

But how to hold the hollow bone,
the fluttering heart, the onyx eye, and downy wing?

Are they keening their terror that spring won't come
for companions gone but not forgotten?

It is not enough. I must remember,
I must speak their names.

Cottonwood Warning

for Emily Dickinson

This dead cottonwood haunts me, warning
take nothing for granted.
Spring is not given to all.
Burgeoning is not a demand
we can make to the gods.
There is no summer glory

for trunks wrapped in Lethe's embrace.
Standing silver among its supple sisters,
did it choose to renounce the effort of blooming?
Or did the cold gods decree,
"This is your time to forget the flutter of
malachite, emerald, jade?"

> *Hope is not the thing*
> *with feathers, but leaves, argent,*
> *reaching for the rain.*

It's About Time

Borne in scalded winter, and starved for sun,
wind bellows roof shingles into whistling hollows.
Brittle icy ledges block the river's run.
Darkness enters early and abides too long.
Swallows hide and robins weep their sad tomorrows.
La Llorona keens her fearful bitter song.

I cast flat stones across the frozen waste,
skittering like spiders along the icy plane.
They seek a haven to break their slippery race,
much as I in my grief have sought the same.
Till forsythia's golden glow turns snow to rain,
I seek solace, awaiting spring and time for grace.

Just as April's light makes new growth visible,
letting go of grief makes all things possible.

Never the Same River Twice

"You can't push the river."
—Chuck Pyle

The river burbles over rock, pebble, sandbed,
buzz of gnat-hatch above
pop of trout rising in a chiaroscuro pool.

There, if I was quiet enough,
the mountain would etch into me
the way the river limned the bank.

That summer, there was only my footfall
at the muddy edge, 'til I ached for human voices,
dreamed my name on a someday lover's lips.

As fall leaves turned
and fell into the chill water,
I returned to the cacophonous city
with its clang and clamor.

The river became a memory,
appeared only in dreams
tentative and green at dusk.

Unable to hear the water's ways,
the city is no less lonely
though full of sounds.
People flow by day and night.

Here, I listen for susurrations in the crowd,
I remember that nothing is more silent
than the pulse and pull of a water-strider
riding a ripple's crest.

I long for the sun's slant on moving water,
a golden dance at the bottom of a rill.

Minnows swirl, their shadows
bunch against the cascade.

Time eddies, a spiral, a thread pulling.
If I return there now,
will the river be different?
Will I?

Flood Pantoum

—Big Thompson Canyon, September, 2013

It's changing my idea of a river,
my green refuge turned roiling molasses.
Waters rushing and rising
like Shiva wreaking destruction as he passes.

My green refuge now roiling molasses!
Strange how mud makes everything clear.
Like Shiva, destroying and cleansing as he passes
those things and places I once held dear.

Strange how mud makes everything clear,
making all this baggage unimportant,
when things and places I once held dear
can change and vanish in an instant.

Making all my baggage unimportant.
I should have cleared this place out years ago.
Life can change and vanish in an instant.
It's people and memories you never quite let go.

I should have cleared out years ago,
before waters came rushing and rising.
Now watching my history vanish in an instant
is changing my idea of a river.

Upon Reflection

Above the harrowed field
too high to smell the newly turned soil,
I watch clouds' white tumult
unfurl across the open plain

like colossal rambling sheep
grazing in the azure arc above.
Cumulus, tipped gold and green,
rest on the water.

It's as if I made this day.
As if they came at my bidding.
As if I wielded god-like power to
link land and lake in this cloud-dance.

Then I spot the hawk,
floating, silent, rufous wingtips up
lifted by air I cannot see nor claim,
at ease surveying his fresh-made kingdom—

cloud, lake, hill, trees—
and in his freedom
I know that I am small.

While Waiting at the Train Crossing

To still my impatience
I imagine myself in tree time,
where I know one place so well
I can tell by the change in minutes of light
what will happen next.

No surprises, no vagile wandering,
just a circle of seasons root and reach
while my rings form, as I anticipate
hummingbirds' return.
I know when the monarchs will arrive.

And when being tree is not slow enough
I try to think in rock time.
I am worn smooth by a river.
I roll, rise, and fall through decades,

my entire human lifetime less than a flutter,
a flit, in my eon-slow slide toward a far ocean.

Not on My Life List

I.
I have seen a red-headed house finch, glossy-necked
grackles with midnight chests,
and purple martins in colors reversed,
though I could not tell you their Latin names.

I know those nasty jays that come
when the robins return every spring—
one blue-crested, the other red-breasted,
all trilling passionately to garner potential mates.

I do not keep a life list
or make birdhouses for martins
who have forgotten how to build their own..
They all come despite the absence of water or seeds.

II.
Last fall, two great owls landed on my
silver cottonwood's ruckled branch,
just at dusk.
Mottled gray and brown, a mated pair,

their movement nearly invisible
among drying leaves
that crackled in the breeze.
For weeks I kept the field glasses close.

III.
Once, the owls came down and bobbled about the yard,
hunting mice, so clumsy,
slow moving, 'til swiftly they launched
back to their almost-hidden perch.

For hours I heard them calling in the dark grove,
first one, then the other answering,
much the way we used to call to each other,
a mated pair walking through woods.

Milkweed

To tread lightly on the earth*
first breathe in and out slowly
to sense how oxygen walks barefoot,
then observe butterflies, so weightless
even our poetry burdens them.
~Malcolm Alexander*

After a year of gray veils,
clutching my loneliness like a rosary
rubbed smooth and familiar,

today a yellow swallowtail
touches down on the milkweed
that has, at last,

bloomed its pink fist open,
a pale planet
bobbing atop a thin green tower.

I have for years cut down this juicy stem,
thinking it an invasive weed
among my purple salvia,

till a green-thumbed friend
described its magnetic effect on the butterflies.
I let it grow.

And this year a giant flicker
of butter-gold filigreed with black lacework
alights and flexes.

The wings pulse   pulse,
 a rhythm matching my heartbeat.
Silently it moves from blossom   to blossom.

I barely breathe, lest it disappear.
Could anything be more alive
in this moment?

Yellow glow brings me home
to mid-summer, to rippling heat, with a joy so full
there is no room for yesterday's grieving.

*from "Beginner's Lesson," by Malcolm Alexander, from prison, 2006. He was wrongfully convicted and jailed for 38 years for a rape he did not commit. He was freed in 2018 due to the efforts of The Innocence Project.

To Know Spring

to know spring
first know winter

wake the pine
know this place

when snowflakes and tulips
pas de deux

winter
loses again

Acknowledgments
I am grateful to the following books and journals in which current or earlier versions of these poems first appeared, and to their editors for supporting my poetry.

Encore – "Great Blue Heron Rising"
Going Deeper – "A Slight Warming Trend"
Mountains, Myths & Memories – "Cottonwood Warning"
Plant-Human Quarterly – "September Morning" and "The Seed's Prayer"
Pooled Ink – "The Language of Crows" and "Flood Pantoum"
Reflections – "Upon Reflection"
Progenitor Journal – "September Morning"
The Mountain – "Never the Same River Twice"
The Paths We Take and *Mountains, Myths & Memories* – "Creation"
A Tribute to Loveland – "Come Rain or Come Shine"

Special Thanks

Thanks to the following friends, writers, editors, and teachers who helped nurture this book into being:

To my poetry mentors: Cynthia and Bill Tremblay.

To the editors who midwifed the manuscript: Kathleen Willard, Veronica Patterson and Karen Betstadt.

To the Daz-Boggians Loveland Poetry Workshop: John, Claudia, Gordon, Shelley, Terry, Shirley, Lynn and Pat.

To The Wolverine Poetry Workshop: Jack, Kathleen, Joan, and Celia.

To Sue Foster, who left this world too soon, and to Kate, Lynda, and Sandy, who all listened.

And always, to Steve.

About The Author

Lorrie Wolfe is an award-winning poet, editor, and technical writer living in northern Colorado. She served as poetry editor for *RISE: An Anthology of Change* (2020 Colorado Book Award Winner), and for *Exception /All, Mountains, Myths, & Memories,* and *Chiaroscuro.*

Lorrie had a poem nominated for the Pushcart Prize in 2023. She was named Poet of the Year at the 2014 Denver Ziggies Poetry Festival. Her chapbook, *Holding: From Shtetl to Santa,* (Green Fuse Press) is available at *Lorriewolfe.com.* Her work has appeared in *The Mountain, Earth's Daughters, Pilgrimage, Pooled Ink, Plant-Human Quarterly* and more.

She maintains an email list of more than 350 Colorado poets and sends out announcements of poetry events nearly every day. Her goal is to support poets and build an audience for live and zoomed events.

She graduated *Magna Cum Laude* from Colorado State University. After many years as a community organizer, she still believes in the power of words to unite and move people, including poets.

Her two-word mantra is "Show up."

Learn more about Lorrie at *lorriewolfe.com*

About The Press

Middle Creek Publishing believes that responding to the world through art & literature—and sharing that response—is a vital part of being an artist.

Middle Creek Publishing is a company seeking to make the world a better place through both the means and ends of publishing. We are publishers of quality literature in any genre from authors and artists, both seasoned and those who are undiscovered or under-valued, or under-represented, with a great interest in works which illuminate or embody any aspect of contemplative Human Ecology, defined as the relationship between humans and their natural, social, and built environments.

Middle Creek Publishing's particular interest in Human Ecology is meant to clarify an aspect of the quality in the works we will consider for publication and as a guide to those considering submitting work to us. Our interest is in publishing works which illuminate the human experience through words, story or other content that connects us to each other, our environment, our history, and our potential deeply and more consciously.